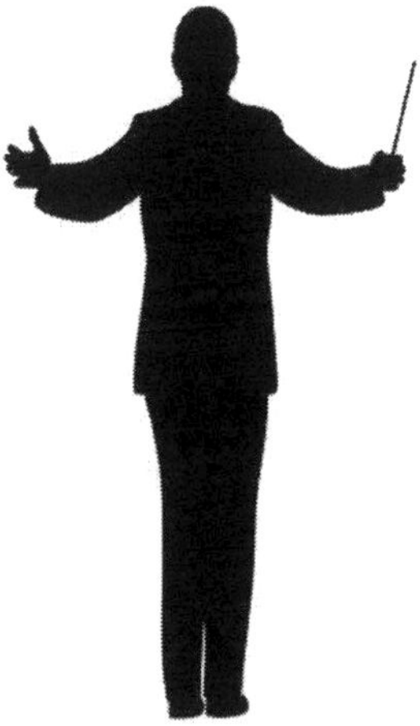

# THE GENERALIST'S ADVANTAGE
# SYMPHONY OF DISCIPLINES JOURNAL

An Intra-Personal Assessment Tool for Empowered Cross-Disciplinary Success

## JOE CURCILLO

The Generalist's Advantage: An Intra-Personal Assessment Tool for Empowered Cross-Disciplinary Success
by Joe Curcillo

Copyright © 2025 by Joe Curcillo

All rights reserved. No part of this book may be used or reproduced in any manner whatsoever without written permission except in the case of brief quotations embodied in critical articles and reviews.

For information, contact:
Synergy Thinkers Press

**Synergy Thinkers Press**

Harrisburg, Pennsylvania
www.TheGeneralistsAdvantage.com

ISBN: 978-1-7324856-3-1 (paperback)

First Edition

Printed in the United States of America

*For the ones who never picked just one lane—
who live in the liminal,
who build bridges between disciplines,
and who know the real magic happens
in the spaces between the notes.*

# Table of Contents

**Preface: Your Life Is a Symphony** .................... 11
**Introduction: Welcome to Your Symphony**............. 15
The Orchestra of You................................ 16
A Journal for Growth................................ 16
Why This Matters................................... 17
Let's Begin......................................... 17

**Chapter 1: The Strings of Your Symphony—Core Skills and Foundations**................................ 19
What Are Your Strings?.............................. 19
Exercise 1: Discovering Your First Violin................ 20
Exercise 2: Exploring Your Second Violin ............... 21
Exercise 3: Finding Your Violas ....................... 22
Exercise 4: Uncovering Your Cellos and Basses........... 24
Bringing Your Strings Together ....................... 25
Your Strings in Action............................... 26

**Chapter 2: Woodwinds—Adding Detail and Depth**....... 27
What Are Your Woodwinds?.......................... 27
Exercise 1: Identifying Your Flutes and Piccolos .......... 28
Exercise 2: Exploring Your Oboes ..................... 29
Exercise 3: Reconnecting with Your Clarinets ............ 31
Exercise 4: Connecting with Your Bassoons.............. 32
Bringing Your Woodwinds Together.................... 33
Your Woodwinds in Action .......................... 35

## Chapter 3: Brass—Adding Boldness and Exploration ..... 37
What Are Your Brass Instruments? ..... 37
Exercise 1: Spotlighting Your Trumpets ..... 38
Exercise 2: Discovering Your Horns ..... 39
Exercise 3: Building Your Trombones ..... 40
Exercise 4: Anchoring with Your Tubas ..... 41
Bringing Your Brass Together ..... 42
Your Brass in Action ..... 44

## Chapter 4: Percussion—Rhythm and Emphasis ..... 45
What Is Your Percussion Section? ..... 45
Exercise 1: Identifying Your Timpani ..... 46
Exercise 2: Exploring Your Drums ..... 47
Exercise 3: Revisiting Your Cymbals ..... 49
Exercise 4: Celebrating Your Xylophone ..... 50
Bringing Your Percussion Together ..... 51
Your Percussion in Action ..... 53

## Chapter 5: The Conductor—Your "Why" and Core Identity ..... 55
What Is Your Conductor? ..... 55
Exercise 1: Discovering Your "Why" ..... 56
Exercise 2: Analyzing Your Journey ..... 57
Exercise 3: Articulating Your Conductor ..... 59
Exercise 4: Living Your "Why" ..... 60
Bringing Your Conductor to Life ..... 61
Your Conductor in Action ..... 63

**Chapter 6: Harmonizing Your Symphony—**
**Cross-Disciplinary Thinking** .......................... 65
What Is Cross-Disciplinary Thinking? .................. 65
Exercise 1: Mapping Your Orchestra ..................... 66
Exercise 2: Discovering Connections .................... 68
Exercise 3: Blending Your Skills ........................ 69
Exercise 4: Implementing Cross-Disciplinary Thinking..... 70
Bringing It All Together................................ 72
Your Symphony in Harmony ............................. 73

**Chapter 7: Sustaining and Refining Your Symphony** ...... 75
The Symphony as a Changing Work ..................... 75
Embracing Lifelong Learning............................ 76
Finding a Balance Between Steadiness and Change ........ 76
Review and Realignment................................ 77
The Importance of Feedback and Teamwork.............. 78
Embracing the Journey ................................. 79

APPENDIX A: The Orchestra Chart..................... 81
APPENDIX B: The Symphony Diagnostic Scorecard....... 83
APPENDIX C: Continuing Your Symphony .............. 89
APPENDIX D: Bonus: Advanced Exercises............... 91
Author's Note ......................................... 93
Explore The Generalist's Advantage Leadership .......... 95
About the Author...................................... 97

# Preface
# Your Life Is a Symphony

We've all been asked, *What do you want to be when you grow up?* And most of us were expected to answer with one thing—one career, one specialty, one path. Pick a lane. Stay in it. Master it. That's the way to succeed, right?

But what if the real key to success isn't about staying in one lane at all? What if the magic—the innovation, the breakthroughs, the ability to truly stand out—comes from moving between disciplines, drawing from multiple skills, and seeing connections that others miss?

This is the power of cross-disciplinary thinking—it's where the real magic happens. When disciplines intersect, barriers dissolve, and entirely new possibilities emerge. This isn't just about innovation; it's about transformation. Whether in your personal growth, professional success, or business strategy, breaking down silos and integrating diverse knowledge allows individuals, teams, and companies to move forward with agility and vision. The future belongs to those who think beyond boundaries, connect ideas, and create something the world has never seen before.

That's where this journal comes in.

*The Symphony of Disciplines Journal* is for the thinkers, the doers, the innovators—the people who refuse to be boxed into a single definition. It's for those who are skilled at one thing but curious about ten more. It's for the person who sees connections where others see barriers. And it's for anyone who has ever felt torn between multiple passions and wondered if it were a weakness when, in reality, it was your greatest strength.

If you've read *The Generalist's Advantage* you already know that being a cross-disciplinary thinker isn't just about knowing a little about a lot—it's about knowing how to integrate those skills, how to pull ideas from one world into another, and how to create something new from the intersections. But if you haven't read that book, don't worry. This one stands on its own. It will walk you through what it means to live in multiple lanes and show you how to bring those lanes together in a way that amplifies everything you do.

This book is structured like a symphony because your life, your expertise, and your experiences play different roles in a larger composition. You have your core skills (your strings), your areas of specialization (your woodwinds), your bold ventures (your brass), and the creative elements (your percussion) that bring rhythm and life to everything you do. And at the center of it all is you—the conductor, the one who brings it all together.

Through exercises, stories, and real-world applications you'll see how to turn what might feel like a collection of unrelated skills into a cohesive, powerful force. You'll learn how to move fluidly between disciplines, how to think beyond the limits of specialization, and how to orchestrate your unique combination of talents into something extraordinary.

So if you've ever felt like you didn't fit neatly into a single box—good. You're exactly who this book was written for. It's time to stop picking just one lane. It's time to step onto the podium and conduct the full symphony of who you are.

Let's make some music.

# Introduction
# Welcome to Your Symphony

Life is a symphony—a beautiful, intricate arrangement of experiences, skills, and passions. Each element plays a unique role: some blend in harmony while others contrast dramatically, adding texture and richness to the overall composition. Together, they create something far greater than the sum of their parts. Like a symphony, your life has sections: core expertise, unique experiences, and those surprising, discordant notes that first seem out of place but later reveal themselves as essential.

This book is an invitation to embrace the symphony within you. It draws upon the principles of the Generalist's Advantage, celebrating the integration of diverse disciplines and experiences to amplify your life's impact. By refining your core skills, weaving together unexpected insights, and leveraging the intersections between fields, you'll discover the transformative power of cross-disciplinary thinking. Whether you're an entrepreneur seeking innovation, a leader balancing complexity, or simply someone navigating the multidimensionality of life, this journal will help you step into the role of conductor—aligning your unique orchestra to create something extraordinary.

The goal isn't just mastery of individual sections but the ability to orchestrate them with intention and clarity. Each skill, experience, and passion adds depth, boldness, or rhythm to your life's composition. As we explore these layers you'll uncover not only the power of being multidimensional but also the freedom that comes from owning your diverse capabilities.

So pick up your baton and embrace the music. Let's compose a masterpiece that is uniquely yours.

## The Orchestra of You

Your life is made up of different sections, just like the instruments in an orchestra:

- **The Strings** represent your foundational skills—the expertise that drives your core identity.
- **The Woodwinds** add nuance, showcasing specialized knowledge and unique roles.
- **The Brass** symbolizes bold ventures and new explorations.
- **The Percussion** punctuates your life with the rhythm of past roles, temporary projects, and creative outlets.
- **The Conductor** represents your "why"—the purpose that ties the orchestra together and gives your symphony direction.

Each element plays a vital role in shaping your identity. The goal isn't to master one section at the expense of the others—it's to recognize how they all work together to create a unified, powerful performance.

## A Journal for Growth

This isn't just a book to read—it's a journal designed to help you grow. Think of it as a tool for uncovering the full range of your talents, refining your skills, and aligning your efforts with your purpose.

Each section builds on the last, guiding you through a process of self-discovery and intentional growth. At the end of every chapter you'll find reflective prompts, questions, and exercises to guide your thinking and bring the concepts to life. There's an orchestra chart in the appendix to help you visualize your symphony. I encourage you to engage deeply with these activities, take notes, and journal your thoughts as you progress. Let this process challenge you to see yourself differently.

The value of this book lies not just in what you learn but in how you apply that learning. This is your opportunity to step up as the conductor of your life.

## Why This Matters

In a world that often celebrates specialization, this book is a reminder of the power of being multidimensional. The more you embrace the intersections of your disciplines, the more adaptable, innovative, and resilient you become. You don't have to fit into one box—you can thrive by celebrating the full range of who you are.

By the end of this journey you'll have a deeper understanding of your skills, your purpose, and how to bring everything together into a harmonious and impactful performance.

## Let's Begin

As you turn the page, approach this book with curiosity and openness. Use it as a guide to think, reflect, and grow. Your symphony is waiting to be fully realized, and only you can conduct it.

Step onto the podium and pick up your baton. Let's discover the music within you.

# Chapter 1

# The Strings of Your Symphony— Core Skills and Foundations

Picture an orchestra without its strings. The performance would feel hollow, missing the richness and depth that make it truly captivating. Strings are the foundation of a symphony, providing its melody, structure, and soul.

Now, think of your life as a symphony. Your **strings** represent the core skills and disciplines that form the foundation of your identity. These are the areas where you've invested your time, effort, and passion—the melody that defines who you are and shapes how you move through the world.

In this chapter, you'll explore your strings: the essential skills and fields that define your foundation. Through guided exercises, you'll uncover your unique melody, reflect on what drives you, and identify how to strengthen and harmonize the core elements of your symphony.

## What Are Your Strings?

Strings are the backbone of your orchestra.

- **First Violin:** Your primary skill or expertise that carries your melody.
- **Second Violin:** A complementary skill that supports and enhances your main expertise.

- **Violas:** Bridging disciplines that connect your core skills to other areas.
- **Cellos and Basses:** Depth skills that provide stability and perspective, even if they're less visible.

Each of these plays a vital role in your life. Together, they form the backbone of your identity and set the tone for everything you do.

## Exercise 1: Discovering Your First Violin

The **first violin** leads your symphony. It represents the skill or area of expertise that defines you most—the melody you carry through life.

## Reflect

Take a moment to think about your primary skill.

- What is the core focus of your work or passion?
- What is the skill or expertise others associate with you?
- Where have you spent the most time honing your abilities?

_____

_____

_____

_____

Answer the following questions here or in a separate notebook:

1. What is your primary skill or core discipline?

2. How does this skill shape your professional or personal identity?
3. How do others recognize this skill in you?

**Examples:**
*For a lawyer, the first violin might be litigation skills. For a teacher, it could be classroom management. For you, it might be problem-solving, leadership, or creative thinking.*

_____

_____

_____

_____

# Exercise 2: Exploring Your Second Violin

The **second violin** doesn't take center stage, but it's essential for harmony. It's the skill or ability that complements and enhances your first violin.

# Reflect

Think about the skills that support your primary expertise:
- What ability makes your primary skill even stronger?
- What secondary area of knowledge do you often rely upon?
- What skill fills gaps in your work or makes you more effective?

_____

_____

_____

_____

Answer the following questions here or in a separate notebook:
1. What skill complements your primary expertise?
2. How does this skill improve or support your first violin?
3. In what situations do you most rely on this complementary skill?

**Examples:**
*A marketer's first violin might be strategy, with a second violin of storytelling to make campaigns more engaging. A teacher's first violin might be classroom management, with a second violin of public speaking to engage parents and colleagues.*

_____

_____

_____

_____

## Exercise 3: Finding Your Violas

The **violas** bridge the melody of the violins with the depth of the cellos, creating connection and harmony. In your symphony, they represent the skills that link your primary expertise to other fields or roles.

## Reflect

Consider the skills that connect different aspects of your life and work:

- What abilities help you bring ideas together across disciplines?
- How do you use your primary and secondary skills to interact with others or solve problems?

_____

_____

_____

_____

Answer the following questions here or in a separate notebook:
1. What bridging skills do you have?
2. How do these skills help you connect your main areas of expertise with other disciplines?
3. How do your violas create harmony in your work or life?

## Examples:

*A scientist might use writing skills to simplify complex research for the public. A manager might use conflict resolution to connect technical teams and leadership.*

_____

_____

_____

# Exercise 4: Uncovering Your Cellos and Basses

The **cellos and basses** provide depth and strength to the orchestra. In your symphony, they represent the skills that ground you and give you perspective. These abilities may not always be visible, but they influence everything you do.

# Reflect

Think about the skills that quietly sustain you:

- What abilities help you navigate challenges?
- Are there skills that provide stability even if they're not in the spotlight?
- What disciplines give you a unique perspective or broader understanding?

_____

_____

_____

_____

Answer the following questions here or in a separate notebook:

1. What depth skills do you rely on to stay grounded?
2. How do these skills influence your primary and complementary areas?
3. How do these abilities help you see the bigger picture?

**Examples:**

*A leader might rely on emotional intelligence to manage relationships, even if it's not the most visible skill. An entrepreneur might depend on time management to effectively juggle multiple projects.*

_____

_____

_____

_____

## Bringing Your Strings Together

Now that you've mapped out your strings, let's look at them as a whole.

## Reflect

Take a step back and consider your string section:

- How do your first violin, second violin, violas, cellos and basses work together?
- Are there any areas where you feel a gap or lack of balance?
- Are there skills you'd like to strengthen or explore further?

## Write

Summarize your string section in a few sentences. Include your primary skill, complementary skill, bridging skills, and depth skills.

**Example Summary:**
*"My string section is built around my primary skill of strategic planning (first violin), supported by my ability to communicate clearly (second violin). I bridge these with storytelling (violas), and I stay grounded with time management and emotional intelligence (cellos and basses). Together, these create a strong foundation for my work as a leader."*

_____

_____

_____

_____

## Your Strings in Action

Your string section forms the foundation of your symphony, but it's not static. It will evolve as you grow, explore new fields, and deepen your expertise. Take time to revisit and refine your strings regularly, ensuring they stay in tune with your goals and aspirations.

By understanding and strengthening your strings, you set the stage for the rest of your symphony. These core elements will guide you as you explore new opportunities, take bold risks, and create harmony in your life.

So take a moment to celebrate your strings—the skills and disciplines that make you you. Write them down, reflect on their power, and begin conducting your symphony with confidence and intention.

## Chapter 2

# Woodwinds—Adding Detail and Depth

While the strings form the foundation of your symphony, the **woodwinds** add color, nuance, and individuality. These instruments infuse personality and texture into the performance, making it more layered and engaging. In your life's symphony, the woodwinds symbolize your **specialized knowledge, unique roles,** and **adaptive skills**—the elements that make your identity distinct and versatile.

This chapter invites you to explore your woodwinds. Through guided exercises, you'll uncover the niche areas where you excel, the unique contributions you've made, and the dormant skills that may be ready to shine again.

## What Are Your Woodwinds?

The woodwinds represent the specialized and adaptive aspects of your identity. These include:

- **Flutes and Piccolos:** Niche expertise and certifications that refine your skills.
- **Oboes:** Unique responsibilities or specialized roles that set you apart.
- **Clarinets**: Skills you've learned formally but don't actively use.
- **Bassoons:** Transitional disciplines that connect past roles to your current work.

_____

_____

_____

_____

Each of these elements enhances your symphony, adding precision, adaptability, and a personal touch.

## Exercise 1: Identifying Your Flutes and Piccolos

The **flutes and piccolos** represent your niche expertise—certifications, advanced skills, or specialized areas of knowledge. These are the sharp, clear notes that add precision and brilliance to your symphony.

## Reflect

Think about the focused areas where you've developed expertise:

- Do you hold certifications, degrees, or advanced training in specific areas?
- What niche skills make you stand out in your field?
- Are there areas in which you've gone above and beyond to gain deep knowledge?

_____

_____

_____

_____

Answer the following questions here or in a separate notebook:
1. What specialized skills or certifications define your expertise?
2. How do these skills enhance your work or set you apart?
3. In what situations do you most rely on this expertise?

**Examples:**
*A project manager might list their PMP certification as a flute. A graphic designer might highlight their expertise in UX/UI design as a piccolo.*

_____

_____

_____

## Exercise 2: Exploring Your Oboes

The **oboes** symbolize unique roles or responsibilities that distinguish you from others. These might include leadership roles, involvement in community projects, or responsibilities that reflect your values and individuality.

## Reflect

Think about the unique ways you've contributed:
- Have you taken on roles that are uncommon or distinct in your field?
- Are you involved in community organizations, charitable efforts, or initiatives outside of work?

- Have you led or contributed to projects that reflect your values and individuality?

_____

_____

_____

_____

Answer the following questions here or in a separate notebook:
1. What unique responsibilities or roles have you taken on?
2. How do these contributions reflect your values or make you stand out?
3. How do your oboes connect you to others or create impact?

**Examples:**
*A scientist leading public outreach on climate change might list this as their oboe. An engineer mentoring students in STEM programs could highlight this role as a meaningful and unique contribution.*

_____

_____

_____

_____

# Exercise 3: Reconnecting with Your Clarinets

The **clarinets** represent skills you've learned formally but don't currently use. These dormant abilities remain part of your repertoire, ready to be activated when needed.

# Reflect

Think about the skills or disciplines you've set aside:
- Are there degrees, certifications, or training you've completed but no longer use?
- Are there skills you haven't applied recently but that still hold value?
- Do you have knowledge in areas outside your current focus?

_____

_____

_____

_____

Answer the following questions here or in a separate notebook:
1. What skills or knowledge have you learned but don't actively use?
2. How might these dormant skills still influence your work?
3. Could these abilities be revived to add value in a new way?

**Examples:**
A business leader with a background in graphic design might list this as a clarinet. A teacher who studied counseling might include this as a skill they could revisit to enhance their work.

_____

_____

_____

_____

## Exercise 4: Connecting with Your Bassoons

The **bassoons** represent transitional disciplines—skills or roles you've shifted away from but that still influence your current work. Like the bassoon's steady, grounding sound, these experiences provide continuity and depth.

## Reflect

Consider the disciplines you've moved away from:

- Have you transitioned from one field or role to another?
- Are there past experiences that still inform how you approach challenges?
- How do these roles connect your past to your present?

_____

_____

_____

_____

Answer the following questions here or in a separate notebook:
1. What transitional roles or skills still influence your work?
2. How have these experiences shaped your perspective or approach?
3. What lessons from these disciplines continue to resonate in your life?

**Examples:**
*A journalist who transitioned to marketing might list storytelling as a bassoon. A teacher who moved into corporate training might include classroom management as a foundational influence.*

_____

_____

_____

_____

## Bringing Your Woodwinds Together

Now that you've explored your woodwinds, let's reflect on how they work together to add character and nuance to your symphony.

## Reflect

- How do your flutes and piccolos (specialized skills) sharpen your performance?
- What role do your oboes (unique responsibilities) play in distinguishing you?
- How do your clarinets (dormant skills) and bassoons (transitional disciplines) provide versatility and depth?

_____

_____

_____

_____

## Write

Summarize your woodwinds in a few sentences. Include your niche expertise, unique roles, and the dormant or transitional skills that influence your work.

**Example Summary:**
*"My woodwinds include my certification in financial planning (flutes), my leadership in a sustainability initiative (oboes), my background in graphic design (clarinets), and my previous experience in sales (bassoons). Together, they add depth, adaptability, and individuality to my work as a business strategist."*

_____

_____

_____

## Your Woodwinds in Action

Your woodwinds bring precision, uniqueness, and flexibility to your symphony. By understanding these elements, you can use them more effectively, whether you're refining your skills, embracing new roles, or reconnecting with dormant abilities.

Take a moment to appreciate the detail and depth your woodwinds add to your life. Write them down, reflect on their significance, and start using these tools to enrich your symphony.

With your strings and woodwinds in harmony, your symphony is already taking shape. Next, let's explore the bold and adventurous **brass section** that energizes your performance.

### Chapter 3

# Brass—Adding Boldness and Exploration

If strings form the heart of your symphony and woodwinds add nuance, the **brass section** brings boldness, drama, and energy. These instruments create moments that stand out and leave a lasting impression. In your life's symphony, the brass symbolizes your **bold initiatives, new ventures,** and **foundational strengths**—the elements that push boundaries and drive you forward.

This chapter will help you explore your brass section. Through guided exercises, you'll uncover the bold projects you're pursuing, the emerging interests that spark your curiosity, and the foundational strengths that sustain your efforts.

## What Are Your Brass Instruments?

Your brass section represents the adventurous and foundational aspects of your life. These include:

- **Trumpets:** New initiatives or daring projects that you're pursuing.
- **Horns:** Emerging interests or fields you're beginning to explore.
- **Trombones:** Side projects or secondary roles that are gaining momentum.
- **Tubas:** Foundational skills that anchor and support all your efforts.

Each brass instrument adds its voice to your symphony, bringing boldness, innovation, and stability.

## Exercise 1: Spotlighting Your Trumpets

The **trumpets** are your bold, attention-grabbing projects or ventures. These are the initiatives that challenge you, excite you, and define your forward momentum.

## Reflect

Think about the bold moves you're making in your life:
- Are you starting a new business, creative project, or venture?
- Have you taken on a challenging role that pushes you outside your comfort zone?
- What initiatives are you most passionate about right now?

_____

_____

_____

_____

Answer the following questions here or in a separate notebook:
1. What bold projects or initiatives are you pursuing?
2. How do these pursuits reflect your values or ambitions?
3. What impact do you hope these projects will have?

**Examples:**

*A software developer launching their first app might list this as their trumpet. A writer working on their debut novel might spotlight this as a bold project defining their current focus.*

_____

_____

_____

## Exercise 2: Discovering Your Horns

The **horns** symbolize emerging interests and areas of exploration. These are the fields, skills, or hobbies you're curious about but haven't fully committed to yet.

## Reflect

Consider what sparks your curiosity:

- Are you exploring a new skill, industry, or area of study?
- Are there hobbies or interests you're beginning to develop?
- What excites you, even if it's still in the early stages?

_____

_____

_____

_____

Answer the following questions here or in a separate notebook:
1. What new interests or fields are you exploring?
2. How do these areas align with your goals or aspirations?
3. What steps could you take to dive deeper into these interests?

**Examples:**
*An HR manager learning data analytics might list this as a horn. A teacher experimenting with podcasting to share educational tips might highlight this as an emerging area of exploration.*

_____

_____

_____

_____

# Exercise 3: Building Your Trombones

The **trombones** represent side projects or secondary roles that are gaining significance in your life. These might have started as small initiatives but are now becoming more prominent.

# Reflect

Think about initiatives that are growing in importance:
- Do you have a side hustle, creative project, or part-time role that's gaining momentum?
- Are there secondary interests that are becoming more central to your life?
- What activities are starting to shape your goals?

Answer the following questions here or in a separate notebook:
1. What side projects or secondary roles are becoming more significant?
2. How are these projects evolving, and what impact are they having?
3. How can you nurture or expand these initiatives?

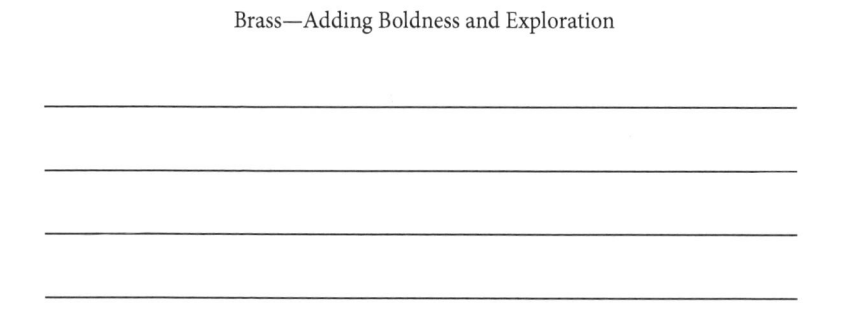

**Examples:**
*A lawyer writing a book might see this as a trombone. A marketing professional teaching online courses in their free time might list this as a secondary role growing in prominence.*

## Exercise 4: Anchoring with Your Tubas

The **tubas** are the backbone of your brass section. They represent the foundational skills and strengths that provide stability, structure, and support for all your efforts.

## Reflect

Think about the abilities that ground you:
- What core skills do you rely on daily, regardless of your role?
- Which abilities are essential for maintaining balance and ensuring success?

- What strengths provide a steady foundation for your bold pursuits?

_____

_____

_____

_____

Answer the following questions here or in a separate notebook:
1. What foundational skills do you consistently rely upon?
2. How do these skills support your more adventurous pursuits?
3. How might you strengthen or refine these abilities?

**Examples:**
*A project manager might list organizational skills as their tuba.*
*A public speaker might highlight adaptability or stage presence as a core competency that anchors their work.*

_____

_____

_____

## Bringing Your Brass Together

Now that you've explored your brass section, let's reflect on how these elements work together to add boldness and stability to your symphony.

## Reflect

- How do your trumpets (bold projects) drive your momentum?
- How do your horns (emerging interests) open new possibilities?
- How do your trombones (side projects) contribute to your growth?
- How do your tubas (foundational skills) anchor and support your efforts?

_____

_____

_____

_____

## Write

Summarize your brass section in a few sentences. Highlight the bold projects, emerging interests, and foundational strengths that define your energy and exploration.

**Example Summary:**
*"My brass section includes launching a sustainable fashion line (trumpet), exploring AI for supply chain solutions (horn), developing a blog on sustainable living (trombone), and relying on negotiation and leadership skills (tubas) to anchor all my efforts."*

## Your Brass in Action

Your brass section is where energy meets exploration. It's the part of your symphony that drives bold action, opens new doors, and sustains your progress. By understanding and embracing these elements, you can confidently pursue the projects and goals that matter most to you.

Celebrate your brass section. Write it down, reflect on its power, and use it to amplify your symphony. With your strings, woodwinds, and brass in harmony, your orchestra is gaining momentum.

Next, we'll explore the **percussion section**, where rhythm, creativity, and past experiences shape your journey.

## Chapter 4

# Percussion—Rhythm and Emphasis

Imagine an orchestra without percussion. It would lack the steady beat that keeps the performance grounded, the dramatic crescendos that demand attention, and the playful accents that surprise and delight. The **percussion section** is the heartbeat of the orchestra, providing rhythm and focus while punctuating key moments.

In your life's symphony, the percussion represents **your past experiences, short-term roles,** and **creative outlets**—the elements that add depth, texture, and rhythm to your journey. These may not always be at the forefront, but they shape how you move forward and navigate challenges.

This chapter will help you uncover the rhythm of your symphony. Through reflection and exercises, you'll explore the roles, projects, and hobbies that have added their unique beats to your life.

## What Is Your Percussion Section?

Your percussion section symbolizes the rhythm and punctuation of your life. These include:

- **Timpani:** Significant past careers or roles that left a lasting impact.

- **Drums:** Short-term projects or temporary roles that influenced your growth.
- **Cymbals:** Disciplines or skills on hiatus that you may choose to revisit.
- **Xylophone:** Creative outlets and hobbies that bring balance and joy.

Each element contributes to your unique rhythm, adding emphasis and meaning to your symphony.

## Exercise 1: Identifying Your Timpani

The **timpani** represent significant past roles—careers or experiences that shaped your identity and still resonate in your life today. These are not just stepping stones; they're the beats that set the foundation for your journey.

## Reflect

Think about the defining roles of your past:

- What past careers or roles have significantly shaped who you are today?
- How did these experiences influence your skills, values, or perspective?
- What lessons from these roles continue to guide you?

_____

_____

_____

_____

Answer the following questions here or in a separate notebook:
1. What are the key roles or careers from your past?
2. How have these experiences shaped your current approach to work or life?
3. What enduring lessons or values did you gain from them?

**Examples:**
*A lawyer who began as a teacher might credit their teaching experience for developing clarity in communication. A business executive who started in customer service might highlight how it taught them empathy and interpersonal skills.*

_____

_____

_____

_____

## Exercise 2: Exploring Your Drums

The **drums** symbolize short-term roles or projects—temporary experiences that may not define your career but added new skills or perspectives.

## Reflect

Consider the short-term experiences that have contributed to your growth:

- Have you taken on temporary roles or freelance projects that taught you something new?

- How did these experiences shape your skills or broaden your perspective?
- Are there lessons from these roles that still influence you today?

_____

_____

_____

Answer the following questions here or in a separate notebook:
1. What short-term roles or projects influenced your growth?
2. How did these experiences add value to your journey?
3. In what ways do they still resonate in your life?

**Examples:**
*A marketer who worked as a barista in college might highlight how it taught them customer service skills. A project manager who briefly freelanced as a designer might credit that experience with sharpening their creative eye.*

_____

_____

_____

_____

# Exercise 3: Revisiting Your Cymbals

The **cymbals** represent disciplines or skills you've paused but may revisit in the future. These are areas that might not be part of your current focus but still hold potential value.

# Reflect

Think about the parts of your life you've set aside:
- Are there skills or roles you've paused but still think about revisiting?
- How might these disciplines add value if you chose to return to them?
- What would it take to reintroduce them into your life?

_____

_____

_____

_____

Answer the following questions here or in a separate notebook:
1. What disciplines or skills have you paused?
2. How might these paused areas contribute to your future goals?
3. What steps could you take to revisit or refine them?

**Examples:**
*An engineer who used to paint might consider picking it up again to enhance their creative problem-solving. A teacher who paused their pursuit of a counseling degree might revisit it as a way to expand their impact.*

## Exercise 4: Celebrating Your Xylophone

The **xylophone** adds playfulness and melody, symbolizing creative outlets and hobbies that bring you joy. These aren't necessarily about productivity—they're about inspiration, balance, and personal fulfillment.

## Reflect

Think about the activities that bring you joy:

- What hobbies or creative pursuits make you feel happy and energized?
- How do these activities inspire your work or bring balance to your life?
- Are there outlets you explore purely for the joy of it?

Answer the following questions here or in a separate notebook:

1. What creative outlets or hobbies bring you joy?
2. How do these activities enhance your well-being or spark new ideas?

3. In what ways do they enrich your life?

**Example:**
*A lawyer who enjoys woodworking might highlight how it provides stress relief. A CEO who plays piano might credit it for sharpening their focus and creativity.*

_____

_____

_____

_____

## Bringing Your Percussion Together

Now that you've explored your percussion section, let's reflect on how these elements create rhythm and balance in your life.

## Reflect

- How do your timpani (significant past roles) influence your present?
- What lessons from your drums (short-term roles) add value to your journey?
- Are there cymbals (paused disciplines) you want to revisit?
- How do your xylophones (creative outlets) bring joy and energy to your life?

_____

_____

_____

## Write

Summarize your percussion section in a few sentences. Highlight the past roles, temporary projects, paused skills, and creative outlets that shape your rhythm.

**Example Summary:**
*"My percussion section includes my early career as a journalist (timpani), a short stint as a freelance copywriter (drums), my paused pursuit of a public speaking certification (cymbals), and my love for photography (xylophone). Together, they give my symphony its rhythm and energy."*

_____

_____

_____

## Your Percussion in Action

Your percussion section is the heartbeat of your symphony. It's where your past experiences, short-term roles, and creative outlets come together to add rhythm, emphasis, and personality. By understanding these elements, you can celebrate their impact, revisit their potential, and use them to keep your symphony moving forward.

Take a moment to appreciate the rhythm your percussion section brings. Write it down, reflect on its importance, and let it guide you as you continue conducting your symphony.

Next, we'll focus on the **conductor**—your purpose—and how it ties your entire symphony together.

## Chapter 5

# The Conductor—Your "Why" and Core Identity

Every orchestra needs a conductor—a unifying force that brings all the instruments together, ensuring each section contributes to the harmony of the performance. Without a conductor, even the most talented musicians can sound chaotic, disconnected, and unfocused. In your life's symphony, the **conductor** represents your **"why"**—the central purpose that gives direction to your actions, aligns your skills, and ties your experiences together into a cohesive whole.

This chapter will help you identify, refine, and embrace your "why." Through thoughtful exercises, you'll uncover the motivation that drives you, explore recurring themes in your life, and learn how to lead your symphony with clarity and intention.

## What Is Your Conductor?

Your conductor is your purpose, the reason behind everything you do. It's the thread that links your skills, experiences, and ambitions, giving your symphony direction and meaning.

Your conductor does three key things:

1. **Provides Clarity:** It helps you understand what drives your decisions and efforts.

2. **Unifies Disciplines:** It connects your diverse skills, ensuring they work in harmony.
3. **Inspires Action:** It keeps you motivated, especially during challenges, by reminding you of your greater purpose.

Without a clear "why," your symphony risks becoming fragmented. A strong purpose, however, allows you to lead with confidence and focus.

## Exercise 1: Discovering Your "Why"

Your "why" is personal and unique, shaped by your values, experiences, and aspirations. Uncovering it requires deep reflection.

## Reflect

Think about what gives your life meaning and motivates you:

- What recurring themes or patterns have emerged in your journey?
- What problems or challenges are you passionate about solving?
- What values or principles consistently guide your decisions?

_____

_____

_____

_____

Answer the following questions here or in a separate notebook:
1. What are the common threads running through your skills and experiences?
2. What motivates you to keep learning, growing, or contributing?
3. How would you describe your purpose in one sentence?

**Examples:**
*A teacher might discover their "why" is "to inspire curiosity and empower students to think critically." A designer might articulate their purpose as "to create beautiful and functional solutions that improve people's lives."*

_____

_____

_____

_____

## Exercise 2: Analyzing Your Journey

Your "why" is shaped by the path you've taken—the challenges you've faced, the lessons you've learned, and the milestones you've reached. Reflecting on these moments can reveal the forces that drive you.

## Reflect

Think about the key moments and lessons from your life:
- What challenges have you overcome and what did they teach you?

- How have your past roles or experiences shaped your current goals?
- What insights have stayed with you through different stages of your journey?

_____

_____

_____

_____

Answer the following questions here or in a separate notebook:

1. What challenges or turning points have influenced your perspective?
2. How have your past experiences shaped your approach to life or work?
3. What lessons or insights do you carry forward into new opportunities?

**Examples:**
*A healthcare professional who overcame personal health struggles might find their "why" in helping others achieve wellness. A former journalist turned author might recognize a recurring theme of storytelling as their driving force.*

_____

_____

_____

_____

# Exercise 3: Articulating Your Conductor

To lead your symphony effectively you need to articulate your "why" in a clear and meaningful way. This will help you stay focused and communicate your purpose to others.

# Reflect

Think about how you would summarize your purpose:
- What is the core mission that ties everything in your life together?
- How do your skills and experiences align with this mission?
- What impact do you want to have on the world?

_____

_____

_____

_____

Answer the following questions here or in a separate notebook:
1. What is your core purpose or mission?
2. How do your skills and experiences contribute to this purpose?
3. Write a personal mission statement that reflects your "why."

**Example:**
*"My purpose is to empower people to think creatively and solve problems collaboratively by connecting diverse ideas and perspectives."*

## Exercise 4: Living Your "Why"

Identifying your "why" is just the beginning—living it is where the magic happens. To bring your purpose to life you need to align your actions with your values and goals.

## Reflect

Think about how you can integrate your "why" into your daily life:

- How do your current roles and activities reflect your purpose?
- Are there areas where you feel out of sync with your "why"?
- What changes can you make to better align with your purpose?

Answer the following questions here or in a separate notebook:
1. How can you align your current work with your purpose?
2. Are there areas where you feel disconnected from your "why"?
3. What steps can you take to more fully live your purpose?

**Examples:**
*A nonprofit leader might prioritize projects that reflect their commitment to social justice. An entrepreneur might focus on initiatives that align with their values of sustainability and innovation.*

_____

_____

_____

_____

## Bringing Your Conductor to Life

Now that you've explored your "why" it's time to reflect on how it ties your symphony together.

## Reflect

- How does your "why" connect your skills, experiences, and goals?
- What steps can you take to align your actions with your purpose?
- How will your "why" guide you through future challenges and opportunities?

_____

_____

_____

_____

## Write

Summarize your conductor in a few sentences. Include your purpose, the lessons that shaped it, and the impact you hope to create.

**Example Summary:**
*"My purpose is to inspire creativity and connection by blending diverse ideas into innovative solutions. This mission is shaped by my journey as a designer and storyteller, and it drives me to create meaningful work that improves lives."*

_____

_____

_____

_____

## Your Conductor in Action

Your "why" is the heartbeat of your symphony. It gives meaning to your skills, structure to your actions, and clarity to your decisions. By understanding and embracing your purpose you can lead your symphony with confidence, ensuring every element works in harmony.

Take a moment to celebrate your conductor. Write it down, reflect on its significance, and use it to guide your symphony forward.

With your strings, woodwinds, brass, percussion, and conductor all aligned, your orchestra is ready to create something extraordinary. Next, we'll bring it all together with **cross-disciplinary thinking**—the key to harmonizing your entire symphony.

# Chapter 6

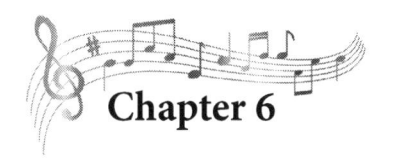

# Harmonizing Your Symphony— Cross-Disciplinary Thinking

Picture an orchestra where each section—strings, woodwinds, brass, and percussion—plays beautifully, but separately.

Without coordination, the performance would feel fragmented, lacking the seamless flow that transforms individual parts into a masterpiece. The secret to brilliance lies in **harmony:** the ability to blend diverse elements into a cohesive and impactful whole.

In your life's symphony, **cross-disciplinary thinking** is the key to harmonizing your skills, experiences, and interests. It's about seeing the connections between seemingly unrelated disciplines, using those intersections to innovate, adapt, and solve complex problems.

This chapter will guide you through the art of cross-disciplinary thinking. Through reflection and exercises, you'll learn how to integrate your unique "orchestra," creating harmony that empowers you to excel in a rapidly changing and interconnected world.

## What Is Cross-Disciplinary Thinking?

Cross-disciplinary thinking goes beyond combining skills. It's about deeply integrating methods, perspectives, and insights from different areas to create something greater than the sum of its parts.

Think of your skills as ingredients:

- A **fruit salad** represents multidisciplinary thinking, where each skill remains distinct but contributes to the whole.
- A **smoothie** represents interdisciplinary thinking, blending skills into a unified result.
- A **cocktail:** Adding tequila or something else from the bar symbolizes cross-disciplinary thinking, combining diverse elements intentionally to create something unique and transformative. Pulling something from a different lane is what creates the magic.

Cross-disciplinary thinking is about being the conductor who knows how to blend these elements in just the right way.

## Exercise 1: Mapping Your Orchestra

To harmonize your symphony you first need to map its components. This means identifying your core skills (strings), specialized knowledge (woodwinds), bold pursuits (brass), and past experiences or creative outlets (percussion).

## Reflect

Take a moment to visualize your orchestra:

- What are the core skills and disciplines that define you?
- What specialized areas or unique contributions add depth and texture?

- What bold projects or exploratory interests bring energy and adventure?
- How do your past roles or creative outlets punctuate your journey?

___

Answer the following questions here or in a separate notebook:
1. What are the key components of your symphony?
2. How do these elements connect or overlap?
3. Are there areas with gaps or missed opportunities?

**Example:**
*"My orchestra includes strategic planning (strings), public speaking (woodwinds), launching a podcast (brass), and painting as a creative outlet (percussion). Together, these elements give my work both structure and flair."*

## Exercise 2: Discovering Connections

Cross-disciplinary thinking thrives on the connections between skills. By identifying links between your disciplines you can uncover new opportunities for innovation and growth.

## Reflect

Consider how your skills and experiences relate to one another:
- How do your hobbies influence your professional work?
- What lessons from past roles still apply to your current challenges?
- Are there areas where combining skills could lead to fresh ideas?

_____

_____

_____

_____

Answer the following questions here or in a separate notebook:
1. What connections exist between your skills, experiences, and interests?
2. How can these links enhance your work or help you solve problems?
3. Are there unexpected intersections that could inspire innovation?

**Examples:**
*A marketer who loves storytelling might use that skill to craft compelling brand narratives. A scientist who enjoys photography*

*might apply visual storytelling to make their research more accessible.*

_____

_____

_____

_____

## Exercise 3: Blending Your Skills

Once you've identified connections, the next step is intentional integration. This means blending your skills to create new approaches, tackle challenges, and stand out in your field.

## Reflect

Think about how you can merge your skills for maximum impact:
- What problems could you solve by combining different areas of expertise?
- Are there projects or roles where you could apply your unique skill set?
- How can you use your varied experiences to approach challenges differently?

_____

_____

_____

Answer the following questions here or in a separate notebook:
1. How can you blend your skills to innovate or solve problems?
2. Are there specific projects where integrating your disciplines would add value?
3. What unique perspective do you bring by connecting your skills?

**Examples:**
*An engineer with storytelling skills might develop better ways to explain complex systems to non-technical stakeholders.*
*A teacher with a background in design might create visually engaging lesson plans to enhance student learning.*

_____

_____

_____

_____

# Exercise 4: Implementing Cross-Disciplinary Thinking

The final step is putting your cross-disciplinary thinking into action. This involves staying curious, collaborating with others, and experimenting with new approaches.

# Reflect

Consider how you can apply cross-disciplinary thinking in your daily life:

- How can you keep learning and exploring new fields?
- Who can you collaborate with to gain fresh perspectives?
- What projects or challenges could benefit from a cross-disciplinary approach?

_____

_____

_____

_____

Answer the following questions here or in a separate notebook:

1. What steps will you take to practice cross-disciplinary thinking?
2. Are there areas where you want to expand your knowledge or skills?
3. How will you measure success in the integration of your disciplines?

**Examples:**
*A project manager might decide to explore behavioral psychology to improve team dynamics. A designer might collaborate with engineers to bring technical depth to their creative work.*

_____

_____

_____

_____

## Bringing It All Together

Now that you've mapped your orchestra, discovered connections, and explored ways to blend your skills, take a moment to reflect on how cross-disciplinary thinking can transform your symphony.

## Reflect

- How does integrating your skills create new opportunities for growth and innovation?
- What challenges can you tackle more effectively by combining disciplines?
- How does cross-disciplinary thinking help you stand out in your field?

## Write

Summarize your approach to cross-disciplinary thinking in a few sentences. Highlight the connections, projects, and goals that will drive your symphony forward.

**Example Summary:**
*"By blending my skills in data analysis, storytelling, and leadership, I can create innovative solutions that engage teams and inspire action. This cross-disciplinary approach allows me to stand out as a dynamic leader and problem-solver."*

_____

_____

_____

_____

## Your Symphony in Harmony

Cross-disciplinary thinking is the key to creating harmony in your life's symphony. By connecting your diverse skills and experiences you can unlock new possibilities, adapt to challenges, and innovate in ways others can't.

Celebrate the intersections of your disciplines. Write them down, reflect on their potential, and start using them to create something truly extraordinary. Your symphony is unique—let it play with boldness, creativity, and purpose.

Next, we'll explore how to sustain and refine your symphony over time, ensuring it evolves as you grow.

**Note:** *Before you complete your journey, turn to the appendix to preview your Symphony Diagnostic Scorecard. It will help you evaluate and align all the sections you've discovered so far.*

# Chapter 7

# Sustaining and Refining Your Symphony

As life goes on, the symphony of your skills and interests changes. New experiences, abilities, and chances shape this work, while shifting situations and preferences introduce new aspects. To keep and improve your symphony, you must regularly evaluate, adapt, and grow, making sure it stays in tune with your goals. In this chapter, we will look at how to maintain a lively and relevant symphony as you develop.

## The Symphony as a Changing Work

A symphony is not a fixed show; it's a lively and changing creation. Likewise, your multidisciplinary identity needs consistent effort and enhancement. As someone with diverse interests, your strength is your ability to adjust and bring new elements together. Understanding that your symphony is never "complete" lets you accept change as a normal part of growing. Consider these questions:

- How have my interests and goals changed in the last year?
- What new skills or areas have I pursued and how can they add to my current symphony?
- Which parts of my symphony no longer fit my goals or beliefs?

By thinking about these questions often, you can make sure that your symphony truly represents your changing self.

## Embracing Lifelong Learning

The most engaging symphonies are those that constantly include fresh ideas. Lifelong learning is essential for maintaining your diverse advantage. Commit to exploring new areas, revisiting old hobbies, and staying curious about your surroundings.

Ways to encourage lifelong learning:

- **Set Learning Objectives:** Find areas of interest or relevance to your current path and set aside time to explore them.
- **Seek Variety in Perspectives:** Read broadly, join discussions across different fields, and participate in workshops that challenge your viewpoint.
- **Try New Things:** Take on new roles, projects, or hobbies to widen your skill set and discover unexpected links.

Lifelong learning keeps your symphony lively and adaptive, ensuring it grows with you.

## Finding a Balance Between Steadiness and Change

Maintaining your symphony needs a balance between honoring your core skills and welcoming change. Steadiness offers support while change encourages new ideas.

Maintain core strengths:

- Regularly practice and improve the skills that form the base of your symphony.
- Dedicate time to activities that strengthen your main area and related fields.
- Look back on past achievements for lessons and motivation.

Welcome new aspects:

- Explore new interests or fields that connect with your values and aims.
- Make room for new growth by moving on from areas that no longer benefit you.
- Combine new abilities into your existing structure for unity.

By balancing steadiness and change, your symphony can stay rooted while also being open to growth.

## Review and Realignment

Taking time to review is important for enhancing your symphony. Set aside time to assess your progress, reconsider your priorities, and adjust your efforts to line up with your long-term vision.

Reflection questions:

- Which aspects of my symphony are thriving now, and why?
- Where do I notice imbalance, and how can I fix it?
- How do my current disciplines align with my values and future goals?

_____

_____

_____

_____

Realignment steps:

- Create a "symphony map" that shows your current disciplines and their connections.
- Find gaps or overlapping areas that could use improvement.
- Set clear targets for the next stage of your journey, focusing on growth and balance.

Review and realignment will keep your symphony a strong representation of who you are and where you aim to go.

## The Importance of Feedback and Teamwork

No musician hones their skills alone. You shouldn't either. Seek feedback and collaborate with others to gain new viewpoints and insights.

Feedback suggestions:

- Share your goals and progress with trusted mentors or peers.
- Seek helpful suggestions in areas where you feel lost or unsure.
- Use feedback to find gaps and chances for improvement.

Collaboration options:

- Team up with people from various fields to discover new ideas.
- Join professional groups or communities that match your interests.
- Take part in joint projects that challenge you.

Getting feedback and working together can enhance your ability to improve and maintain your work over time.

## Embracing the Journey

Keeping your work alive and improving it isn't a job to finish but a process to enjoy. Each experience adds depth to your piece. Each challenge sharpens your abilities. Understand that the appeal of your work is in how it changes and grows. As you continue, make sure to:

- Celebrate growth, no matter how little.
- Stay curious and ready for new opportunities.
- Believe in your skills to adapt and harmonize different elements.

Your symphony is uniquely yours—a living, breathing masterpiece that grows and evolves with you. By sustaining and refining it with intention you ensure it continues to resonate with purpose and fulfillment throughout your life.

Let your diverse experiences create a lasting sound. Your work is just starting and the options are boundless. As life unfolds, the symphony of your disciplines evolves. New experiences, skills, and opportunities shape the composition while changing circumstances and interests bring fresh instruments into the fold. To sustain and refine your symphony you must continually assess, adapt, and evolve, ensuring it remains harmonious and aligned with your aspirations.

As you review your growth and prepare for what's next, use the Symphony Diagnostic Scorecard in the appendix to guide your next rehearsal. It's your tool for aligning performance with purpose.

Let the music of your multidisciplinary journey play on. Your symphony has only just begun and the possibilities are limitless.

# APPENDIX A
## The Orchestra Chart

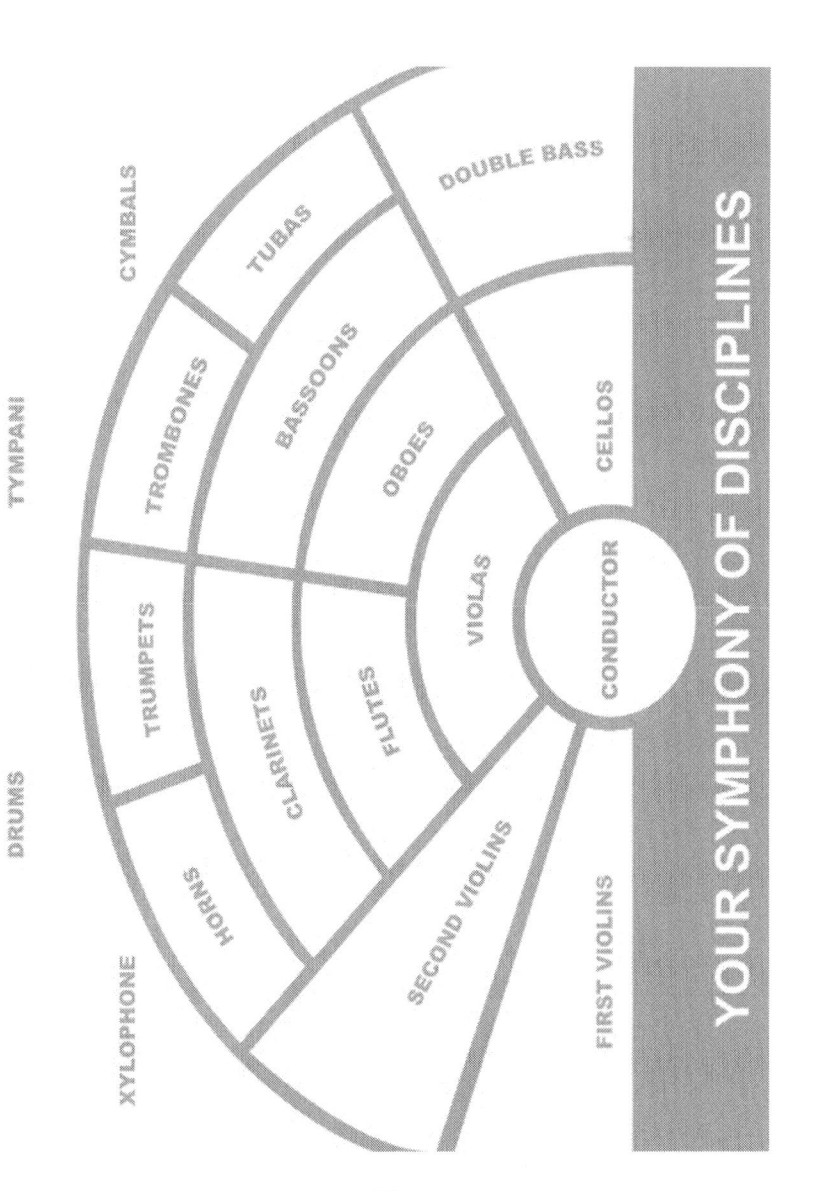

**YOUR SYMPHONY OF DISCIPLINES**

- CONDUCTOR
- FIRST VIOLINS
- SECOND VIOLINS
- VIOLAS
- CELLOS
- DOUBLE BASS
- FLUTES
- OBOES
- CLARINETS
- BASSOONS
- HORNS
- TRUMPETS
- TROMBONES
- TUBAS
- CYMBALS
- TYMPANI
- DRUMS
- XYLOPHONE

# APPENDIX B

## The Symphony Diagnostic Scorecard
*An Application of The Generalist's Advantage*

## Conduct Your Life with Intention

This appendix offers you something new: a baton, a mirror, and a map. Up to this point, you've discovered the sections of your personal orchestra—your Strings, Woodwinds, Brass, Percussion, and Conductor. Now it's time to listen more deeply and ask:

- Are all sections playing in harmony?
- Is your Conductor clearly guiding the music?
- Are any instruments out of tune—or being underutilized?
- Are you ready for your next crescendo?

Inspired by the principles in The Generalist's Advantage, this diagnostic framework lets you assess, align, and amplify the symphony you've been building.

## 1. The Orchestra Scorecard

Evaluate each section of your orchestra using the scale below. You're not judging—you're tuning.

| Section | What's Playing | Strength (1–5) | Alignment with Why (1–5) | Adjustments to Make |
|---|---|---|---|---|
| Strings | Core disciplines and foundations | | | |
| Woodwinds | Specialized knowledge and nuance | | | |
| Brass | Bold ventures and energizing challenges | | | |
| Percussion | Past roles, short-term projects, creativity | | | |
| Conductor | Your purpose—your "why" | | | |

Instructions:

- Strength: How actively does this section contribute to your life's melody?
- Alignment: Is it in sync with your long-term purpose?
- Adjustments: What needs to be tuned, scaled, or shifted?

## 2. Mapping Hidden Harmonies

This is where the symphony becomes more than the sum of its parts.

**Ask yourself:**

- Where do sections support each other naturally?
- Are there combinations you haven't tried yet?
- Where might creative tension become breakthrough?

Write Your Harmony Insights Here:

_____

_____

_____

_____

**Example:**
*"My ability to coach (Strings) is amplified by my storytelling (Woodwinds), while my background in theater (Percussion) adds presence and flair to public presentations."*

## 3. The GAP Ensemble (Generalist Alignment Points)

**You are not just a collection of instruments—you are a conductor managing capacity, energy, and potential.**

| Instrument or Skill | Purpose Score | Engagement Level | Activation Readiness | Action to Take |
|---|---|---|---|---|
| e.g., Visual storytelling | High | Medium | High | Use more in strategic planning |

Definitions:

- Purpose Score: Does this connect to your "why"?
- Engagement Level: Do you feel alive when you use it?
- Activation Readiness: Can you bring it into play now?
- Action to Take: Tune, amplify, pause, or reassign it.

## 4. The 3-2-1 Rehearsal Plan

To refine your performance, let's set a focused rehearsal schedule:

**Three Skills or Instruments to Strengthen:**

1. _____
2. _____
3. _____

**Two Connections to Explore or Strengthen:**

1. _____
2. _____
3. _____

**ONE Bold Cross-Disciplinary Experiment to Launch:**
**Example:**
*"Strengthen emotional intelligence, visual facilitation, and systems thinking. Connect marketing with learning design. Launch a storytelling-based leadership workshop."*

## 5. Encore: Your Symphony Is Alive

This isn't your final performance—it's just your next movement.

By returning to this scorecard regularly you'll become not just a skilled musician, but a masterful conductor. You listen. You adjust. You evolve. You orchestrate new magic.

Appendix B

**Final Prompts:**

- Where are you currently in harmony?
- What feels out of tune?
- What's your next crescendo?

Write your response, and then ... pick up your baton.

_____

_____

_____

_____

_____

_____

_____

Your symphony is waiting.

# APPENDIX C

## Continuing Your Symphony
## Reader's Next-Steps Guide

**Congratulations on completing *Symphony of Disciplines!***

Your journey as a cross-disciplinary thinker is just beginning. Here are your next steps to bring your symphony to life:

## Reflect

Think about your journey so far.

- What parts of your symphony feel strongest right now?
- Where do you want to grow next?

_____

_____

_____

_____

# Step 1: Plan Your Next 90 Days

## Reflect

What two disciplines do you want to intentionally blend?

_____

_____

_____

_____

## Action

- Month 1: Map your skills. Blend two disciplines intentionally.
- Month 2: Launch a "fusion project" combining different skills.
- Month 3: Reflect, adjust, amplify.

## Step 2: Daily Connections Journal

## Challenge:

Each day, write down one connection you see between two unrelated areas.

*(Example journal space)*

Date: _____ | Connection: _____

Date: _____ | Connection: _____

Date: _____ | Connection: _____

## Step 3: Share Your Symphony

## Reflect

Who are three people you could share your unique symphony with?

*(Names or groups)*

_____

_____

_____

_____

# APPENDIX D

## Bonus: Advanced Exercises

### Advanced Exercise 1
### Reverse Engineer a Fusion

### Challenge:
- Find an innovation you admire.
- List what disciplines you think it combines.
- How can you use this method yourself?

_____

_____

_____

_____

### Advanced Exercise 2
### Cross-Disciplinary Deep Dive

### Challenge:
- Pick a discipline you know little about.
- Spend one week studying it.
- Brainstorm new ideas using it!

_____

_____

_____

_____

# Advanced Exercise 3
# 24-Hour Fusion Sprint

## Challenge:

Create something in ONE day by merging three skills you have. What will you create?

_____

_____

_____

_____

# Author's Note

Thank you for taking this journey with me.

Writing Symphony of Disciplines was a labor of love—a way to honor a simple but powerful truth:

*The intersections of your skills, experiences, and passions are not accidents. They are the map to your greatest potential.*

Throughout my own life—from the courtroom to the boardroom, from magic shows to strategic planning sessions—I discovered that the real breakthroughs don't happen when we stay in our lanes.

They happen when we dare to blend, to cross, to orchestrate. I wrote this book for you: the innovator, the explorer, the one who refuses to be confined by a single definition.

As you move forward, I want you to remember:

**You are not limited by your job title, your degree, or even your past.**

**You are limited only by the boundaries you choose to accept—and you are capable of choosing a much bigger stage.**

Keep pushing.
Keep blending.
Keep harmonizing.
Create music that only you can create.

Stand boldly at the crossroads of your talents.
Be the most interesting, dynamic, and unexpected person in any room.

Before you close this book, I invite you to make a personal commitment:

## Reflect

How will you continue orchestrating your symphony moving forward?

_____

_____

_____

_____

Stay bold.
Stay curious.
Stay orchestrated.
Your symphony is only just beginning.

*Joe Curciflo*

# Explore
## The Generalist's Advantage Leadership Suite

### The Journey Doesn't End Here

The Generalist's Advantage Leadership Suite is a connected body of work designed to help leaders think across systems, lead through complexity, and hold the human horizon steady through accelerating change.

The suite includes:

**The Generalist's Advantage: How to Harness the Raw Power of Cross-Disciplinary Thinking.** This flagship book explores the joy of being a generalist and encourages you to break out of your own silos and improve all aspects of your life.

**Symphony of Disciplines: The Symphony of Disciplines Journal** An Intra-Personal Assessment Tool for Empowered Cross-Disciplinary Success.

Your guide to unlocking multidimensional thinking for fully integrated leadership across disciplines, identities, and experiences.

## Hold the Horizon: Lead from the Liminal into the Fog
## The Generalist's Advantage Tactical Field Guide for Leading Across Silos, Systems, and Uncertainty

This is your tactical field guide for leading through silos, systems, and uncertainty—designed for the ones who see more, hold more, and lead when the path ahead is anything but clear.

## Human at the Helm: Harnessing the Generalist's Advantage™: Executive Leadership in the Age of AI

In a world racing toward automation, *Human at the Helm* offers leaders a clear, steady guide to navigating AI with judgment, humanity, and confidence.

Each book stands on its own.
Together, they form a living framework for human-centered leadership built for a complex world.

The future still needs generalists.
It still needs system-sense-makers.
It still needs humans at the helm.

**Learn more at www.TheGeneralistsAdvantage.com**

# About the Author

**Joe Curcillo: The Maestro of
Integration and Cross-Disciplinary Thinking**

Joe is the author of *The Generalist's Advantage: How to Harness the Raw Power of Cross-Disciplinary Thinking*. In a world that demands innovation and adaptability, Joe Curcillo has dedicated his life to transforming diverse skills into strategic solutions for leaders and organizations. With a career spanning law, engineering, entertainment, and business leadership, Joe has spent decades solving complex problems and inspiring innovation through cross-disciplinary thinking.

As a celebrated trial attorney, strategic advisor, and acclaimed speaker, Joe has empowered countless individuals and teams to turn chaos into clarity and thrive in high-pressure environments. His unique ability to bridge disciplines has earned him recognition as a thought leader in leadership development, creative problem-solving, and professional growth.

Joe is also a fine artist, magician, and storyteller who believes every skill—no matter how unrelated it seems—plays a critical role in crafting a meaningful life. This belief forms the foundation of his mission: helping leaders and organizations orchestrate their own symphonies of success.

He lives near Hershey, Pennsylvania, with his wife and an endless supply of caffeine, always ready to explore new intersections of creativity and strategy.

Joe continues to explore new intersections of creativity and strategy, sharing his insights through speaking, coaching, and his books. His work inspires leaders to embrace their multifaceted identities and thrive in an ever-changing world.

Made in the USA
Columbia, SC
26 June 2025